THIS IS MY WISH FOR YOU

TEXT BY CHARLES LIVINGSTON SNELL

COMPILED BY HAROLD DARLING

BORDERS BY DANIEL MACLISE, R.A.

LAUGHING ELEPHANT
MMVII

COPYRIGHT © 1992, BLUE LANTERN STUDIO
ISBN 1-59583-058-8
ISBN13 978-1-59583-058-6

SECOND PRINTING - SECOND EDITION PRINTED IN CHINA ALL RIGHTS RESERVED

THIS TITLE IS ALSO AVAILABLE IN A LARGER EDITION.

LAUGHING ELEPHANT BOOKS
3645 INTERLAKE AVENUE NORTH SEATTLE WA 98103

WWW.LAUGHINGELEPHANT.COM

This is
my
wish
for you...

That the spirit
of beauty
may continually
hover about you
and fold
you close within
the tendernesses
of her wings.

That each
beautiful
and gracious
thing in life
may be unto you
as a symbol
of good for your
soul's delight.

That sun-glories

and
star-glories

9

leaf-glories
and
bark glories

flower-glories

13

and glories
that lurk
in the grasses
of the field

*glories of
mountains*

*and
oceans*

of little streams
of running
waters

glories
of song

of poesy

25

*of all
the arts*

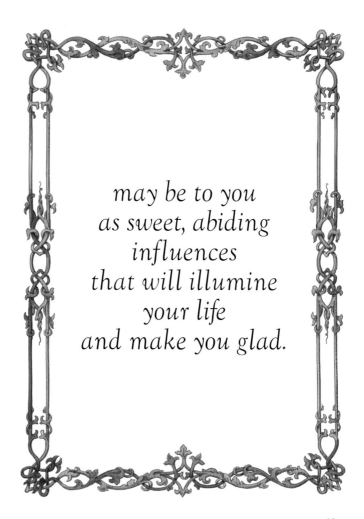

may be to you
as sweet, abiding
influences
that will illumine
your life
and make you glad.

29

That your soul
may be as an
alabaster cup,
filled to
overflowing with
the mystical wine
of beauty
and love.

That happiness
may put
her arms
around you,

33

*and wisdom
make
your soul serene.*

35

This is
my wish
for you.

THIS BOOK WAS DESIGNED AND SET IN GOUDY OLDSTYLE BY
THE BLUE LANTERN STUDIO.
PRINTED IN CHINA THROUGH COLORCRAFT LTD.

PICTURE CREDITS

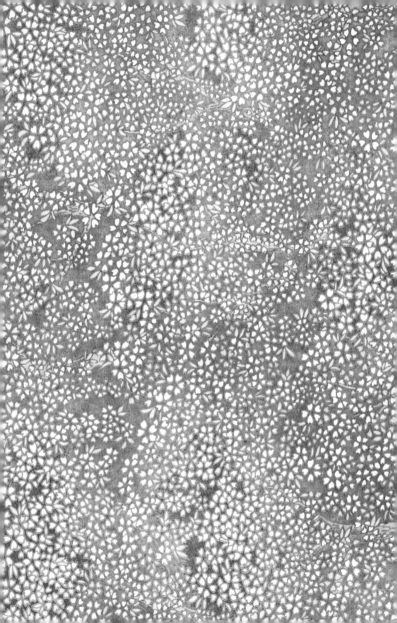